I0470340

Forex Trading Crash Course

• The #1 Beginner's Guide to Make
Money with Trading Forex in 7 Days or
Less! •

By Frank Richmond

Disclaimer

Please note that the information contained within this book is for educational purposes only. Every attempt has been made to provide accurate, up to date and reliable complete information. No warranties of any kind are expressed or implied. Readers acknowledge that the author is not engaging in the rendering of legal, financial, medical or professional advice. The content of this book has been derived from various sources. Please consult a licensed professional before attempting any techniques outlined in this book.

By reading this book, the reader agrees that under no circumstances is the author responsible for any losses, direct or indirect, which are incurred as a result of the use of information contained within this book, including, but not limited to errors, omissions, or inaccuracies.

Table of Contents

Niche Trading for the Curious

Of all the trading markets you might choose to dabble with, the Forex market is arguably the least understood and the most complicated. Ask a layman stock trader and they'll likely tell you that the Forex marketplace is no different to the rest of the stocks and shares. Some might say it's more obscure and baffling than regular trading, but essentially the same sort of deal.

Others might mention that a lot of traders stay away from the Forex market, because it's too unpredictable to tackle with a magic bullet, needs the background training of an economist to understand and is rigged by the world's governments and central banks.

Ask an expert in Forex and they'll give you a very different answer. They'll tell you that it's an ideal place to trade if you are a strategic thinker who is capable of modifying their thinking to match certain key factors: your profit needs, the risk of a trade and the timing.

They'll also explain that Forex is extremely specific in its features. Unlike most markets, it trades throughout the day on six days of the week. It also has the highest leverage of all the markets and involves more than one currency.

They may also pause to reassure you that rigging the Forex system is well nigh impossible thanks to the sheer speed of the market and that you really don't need a degree in economics to find your way through its intricacies – just a curiosity about what's going on in the world's markets and a basic understanding of the rules that govern Forex trading.

So while it is true that Forex trading is a more complicated proposition than simple stocks and shares, it's also a great way to make long term investments that bear fruit you'll appreciate along the way.

Where Does the Forex Market Fit In?

Perhaps the first thing a fledgling trader needs to understand about the Forex market is that it underpins our lives on a daily basis, influencing the purchasing and sales decisions of individuals and businesses right across the world. It's based on currency exchange rates, which is something you'll be aware of if you've travelled abroad even for a weekend vacation.

Any person who crosses a border will need access to the currency of that new country. It's on every vacation check list: get hold of some cash in the currency used at our destination.

Changing that currency is a small scale example of what's happening all day every day. As you can no doubt imagine, the state of one's own currency compared to that of another nation in which one would like to do business is a very important factor. If that country's currency moves downwards compared with yours, it's likely a good time to trade. If it moves up, which means you'll get less for your money, it's less of a juicy proposition.

Now consider just how much trade goes on between countries, from food stuffs to raw energy products and beyond. Every one of those trades is affected by the foreign currency market, because the number of yen, pounds or rubles you are paid will convert into a different number of dollars once the trade is complete depending on what that market is doing.

All countries have their own currency, aside from the group of European nations that have combined their finances to enter into the Euro. It's how we have represented wealth in a tangible manner for at least the last 10 millennia, if historians are to be believed. The value of these currencies, when compared to other currencies, rise and fall constantly. This value is influenced by market forces across the planet.

The Forex market is based on the idea of predicting in which direction these currencies are going to move. Is the yen going to rise or fall in value compared to the Euro? Is the Swiss franc going to rise or fall in value compared to the Great Britain pound? At its heart, it is intended to be a simple way for companies, banks, government entities and whole countries to convert their money from one currency to another. Trillions of US dollars move through it on a daily basis.

Entering into the Forex market means taking your place alongside others with an interest in world currencies. Corporations buy and sell currencies in order to make their trades on imports and exports and also to hedge their bets for the future and for acquisitions and mergers. International banks assist in managing the billions of dollars in transactions that are taking place in the corporate sphere, often trading on the market themselves and on behalf of their clients. National banks take responsibility for managing the economy by shouldering the responsibility for their own currency, sometimes stepping into the market to manipulate that currency to reduce its volatility and protect the stability of the country in the process.

And then there are the speculators – the role you are aiming to take on. Your aim is not to create the most profitable trade for your corporation or keep your country's economy stable. Your goal is simply to make a profit from analyzing the market and its movements. Unlike the big players, such as hedge funds and currency overlay managers, your participation will be small scale and aim to generate the personal profit you are hoping for.

Understanding the Jargon

As with most specialized areas, the Forex market comes with its own terminology that can be utterly undecipherable to the uninitiated. Before we discuss how to trade in Forex, let's get you acquainted with those words and phrases to help you navigate the information more easily.

- Bid Price: This is the price that a buyer is willing to pay for a trade on the market.

- Ask Price: This is the price that a seller is willing to accept for a trade on the market.

- Spread: This is the difference between the bid and ask price and is where the broker makes their money. The more volatility in the market, the wider the spread is likely to be.

- Exchange Rate: A familiar term for vacationers, this refers to the value of one currency in terms of another. For instance, how many Euros you would get for one Australian dollar.

- **Currency Pairs**: The Forex market does not deal with individual currencies, but with pairs of them. For example, the U.S. dollar combined with the Canadian dollar. Some are much more widely traded than others.

- **Cross Currency**: A trade in which neither currency is the U.S. dollar.

- **Cross Rate**: A currency exchange rate between two currencies in which neither are the official currency of the country in which that rate is given. For instance, if an American publication quoted an exchange rate for the Canadian dollar and the Japanese yen.

- **G7 and G20**: These seven countries – the United States, Italy, Japan, France, Germany, Canada and the United Kingdom – are the countries with the most major economic developments and represent over two thirds of the world's wealth. Their currencies are stable, creating currency pairings that have high volume and volatility. The G20 includes these countries but also others including China, India, Argentina, Australia, South Africa, South Korea, Mexico, Saudi Arabia, Turkey,

Brazil and the European Union. These together make up four fifths of the world's trade and 85 percent of the gross domestic product on the planet. These currencies are the ones you will focus on as a trader.

- **Restricted Currencies**: Some governments do not allow trading or speculation with their currencies. This can be because there is a limited availability, concern about the effect of speculation or a desire to control foreign investment.

- **Pip**: This refers to the smallest possible increment by which a currency can move in price. Some currencies are quoted to four or five decimal places, so a pip refers to 0.0001 or 0.00001 of that pound, franc or Euro. Others are quoted only to two decimal places, so a pip is 0.01.

- **Volume**: In Forex trading, this refers to the number of units being traded at one time. One currency may only have five or ten transactions taking place on it over the course of a day, while another may have thousands upon thousands. The former therefore has a low volume of trade, while the latter has a high volume.

- Volatility: This refers simply to how much change there is in the trading price of a currency over time. The more that price changes, the more volatile that currency is said to be.

- Margin: If you don't have enough money to invest in a trade, you can get a secured loan from your broker to increase your capital. This is known as using margin. Doing so involves a great deal of risk as, if the trade is not successful, you will find yourself in significant debt.

- Margin call: This term refers to your broker requiring you to settle your account, usually when a trade reaches a certain level of risk.

- Futures Contract: Contracts that fluctuate as the forex rate moves.

The Decentralized Trading Market

It's important to understand that the Forex market is a decentralized trading market. No regulatory body oversees the overall currency system because that would involve taking charge of the currencies of every country in the world.

Instead, every country has its own currency and its own national, central or federal banks to regulate the financial market.

Why is this crucial to know? Because it means that a broker can offer you an investment opportunity in currency trades without needing to register in every single country. They need only follow the regulations that have been set up in their own country.

This means that there is no central location for Forex trades, though like most forms of trading it does have centers in places such as the New York Stock Exchange. One is able to buy and sell through many different dealers, all of whom are dealing with different banks based on what's known as the "interbank system".

The Interbank Market exists online and is a system that allows currency to be traded between banks and other financial institutions. It's generally reserved for large customers, including governments, and is responsible for around half of the trades on the Forex markets. The trades taking place are usually at a minimum value in the millions and often reach the billions of dollars.

Those dollar amounts far exceed what the average, everyday trader wants to deal in and that can make a beginner feel like there's no real way to get involved. Actually, that's not true – the decisions you make have the potential to influence the market, nudging it further in one direction or the other.

Trading Times

The fundamental motion of the Forex market is somewhat different to other types of trading markets. To put it poetically, Forex follows the sun as it travels around the globe, with particular markets opening and closing according to time zones.

Individual countries open at individual times, with the day starting in New Zealand as its citizens wake up for the day, followed by Sydney and then Tokyo and Hong Kong. As the hours move on, more markets open as those countries wake up for the day and then begin to close as the day ends across the globe.

- The Asian Session opens first with Toyko opening at 8 p.m. Eastern Standard Time and includes currencies from countries such as Australia, Japan and New Zealand. It's generally regarded to be the quietest of all the sessions in terms of how much trading goes on.

- The European Session opens next, with London opening at 3 a.m. Eastern Standard time. This session, obviously, includes all the countries on the European continent. It is the busiest of all the sessions because London is the financial capital of the world.

- The U.S. Session opens last, with New York opening at 8 a.m. Eastern Standard Time. This, too, is a busy session because it can often involve announcement and news that will have a large effect on the dollar.

The three sessions overlap, so you'll find that there are some hours of the day in which two are running at once. Understanding which of the three main markets you'll be dealing with requires first figuring out at what time of day you are free to trade on a regular basis (i.e. when you are not working, sleeping or fulfilling other responsibilities) and which markets are open at that time. If you have your eye on a particular session or market, on the other hand, you will need to adapt your schedule to suit.

The best times to trade are, of course, the times when there are overlaps, because this is when the most volume of trade is taking place, more liquidity is available and there is more volatility. Perhaps the best time of all is at around 1 p.m. Greenwich Mean Time, which is when the UK and European markets are trading and the New York market is just opening. For two hours, these major markets will all be trading together.

A key piece of insight for a Forex trader is that all things are not equal across the hours of the day. A currency that is trading heavily during the Asian Session will not necessarily be trading heavily during the U.S. session. In fact, it will probably not be trading that much at all, because the corporations and governments who deal in international trade are snoozing on their pillows.

Which currencies become your trading bread and butter will therefore depend on where you are in the world and how your daily schedule tends to look. To become a successful trader may mean making concessions to the markets in terms of your own time. In other words, though it might be most convenient for you to do your trading in the couple of hours after you get home from work, that might not be a time when sessions are overlapping and the markets you want to trade in are awake and working.

As an example, let's assume that you are able to be active during the London session. During this time, there is a wide range of trading going on, with around two fifths of the trades concentrating on the pairing of the Euro and U.S. dollar and just under a quarter on the British pound paired with the U.S. dollar. Only a fifth of the trades involve the Japanese yen – down considerably from during the Toyko session, in which it took up three quarters of the trading.

Clearly, where you are and when you are trading is important – and you're going to need to think locally. Wherever the focus of the market is at any particular time during the day is also going to be where the focus of the trading is centered. It might be a poetic way of putting it, but Forex trading really is all about where the sun is shining – and who it's shining on.

You will therefore need to study your options and decide what time of day for you is going to complement your trading the best. More markets open means more active trading and therefore more liquidity on the currencies involved in those markets.

Paired Currencies

For most beginners, the most complicated aspect of Forex trading is not the volatility of the markets, but understanding how currency trading actually takes place and how to dip your oar into its waters.

The common mistake is to assume that it's a simple form of trading because it's top level – you're not dealing in what money can buy, you're dealing in the money itself. However, the market does not actually work with individual currencies.

Instead, it works with what are known as "currency pairs". While there are only around 180 currencies in the world, these can be paired in literally thousands of different ways because, as we're about to find out, it matters which order they are paired in and therefore whether you are dealing with GBP/USD or USD/GBP.

For instance, you might be working with the British pound and the U.S. dollar, a pair referred to as GBP/USD. You could be working with the New Zealand dollar and the U.S. dollar together, which would be referred to as NZD/USD.

Along with the pairings is the meaning associated with their order. It does, indeed, matter which currency is listed first in a pair and which is listed second.

The first currency listed in the pairing is the "base currency". It always represents a total of one and therefore is the stable base on which a trade is found. The base currency is used to figure out the answer to, "One of these equals X amount of that". In other words, if GBP is the base currency, one British pound is equal to X yen, X Canadian dollars and so on.

The second currency listed in the pairing is the "quote currency", and this is the one that alters to reflect the relationship between the two currencies in the pairing. The higher it is, the more of that second currency you will receive if you trade it with some of the base currency. For instance, if one GBP equals 1.4 USD, then for every British pound you trade you will receive $1.40 in American dollars.

This is where the jargon starts to get complicated. When you trade on the Forex market, you will either "bid" or "offer/ask".

- To bid means that you are selling the base currency in the left side of the pairing in exchange for the quote currency on the right hand side of the pair. In other words, you are buying the base currency and selling the quote currency.

- To offer/ask, you will buy the base currency on the left of the pair in exchange for selling the quote currency in the right hand side of the pair. In other words, you are selling the base currency and buying the quote currency.

It's absolutely crucial to memorize the difference between a bid and an ask, because what you'll get out of a trade depends entirely on the relationship between the two currencies. Get it the wrong way round and you'll make a loss where you thought you were making a profit.

You will also need to know that the Forex market specifically deals with how the value of the two currencies in a pair are changing. If the value of one is increasing, however, it doesn't necessarily mean that the other is decreasing. Though the two are paired in the trade, they are not solely going to be influenced by each other – you are simply removing two small cogs from the giant machine and holding them up against each other at a particular moment in time. What's happening in the rest of the machine (and, indeed, what's happening to that cog itself) is also going to influence its value.

The speed at which the two currencies are changing is also not always going to match. Just because the U.S. dollar is increasing fast in value doesn't mean the Canadian dollar is increasing at the same rate. This is where knowledge of the currency market comes into play. Simply looking at the pairing isn't going to tell you much about how it's going to look later in the day when certain markets close. You will need to look at the overall trend of the individual currencies to figure that out.

Obviously, the clearest trades are going to happen when one currency is weakening against the other, allowing you to buy or sell the weak currency at a great price. However, you can also make profit when both are strengthening, if they are doing so at different speeds. We'll talk more about that later in the book.

Choosing Your Currency Pairs

When we mentioned in the previous chapter that there are thousands of possible currency pairs, it may have seemed daunting. Worry not: only a few of these possible pairs form the basis of Forex trading.

Ultimately, the Forex market is dominated by just eight currencies, which doesn't seem a lot. These are the American dollar (USD), the British pound (GBP), the Canadian dollar (CAD), the New Zealand dollar (NZD), the Australian dollar (AUD), the Japanese yen (JPY), the Euro (EUR) and the Swiss franc (CHF).

The first of the pairs are known as the "major" pairs, which are the most heavily traded on the market and tend to get the most focus overall. These are:

- EUR/USD – The Euro against the U.S. dollar
- GBP/USD – The British pound against the U.S. dollar
- USD/CHF – The U.S. dollar against the Swiss franc
- USD/JPY – The U.S. dollar against the Japanese yen.

Following this is the second level of pairs, which are:

- USD/CAD – The U.S. dollar against the Canadian dollar
- AUD/USD – The Australian dollar against the U.S. dollar
- NZD/USD – The New Zealand dollar against the U.S. dollar.

Next we have a set of cross currency pairs that do not involve the U.S. dollar, unlike all the ones we've looked at so far:

- GBP/JPY – The British pound against the Japanese yen
- EUR/JPY – The Euro against the Japanese yen
- EUR/GBP – The Euro against the British pound.

Also bear in mind that, partly due to the fact that it will suit your schedule and partly because you'll be exposed to more news and information about it without having to really try, you'll probably find yourself most comfortable trading in your own home currency. If that happens to fall into one of the major categories, fantastic. If not, consider including it but branching out as much as you are able.

Let's take a closer look at some of these important currencies and the role they play in the Forex market:

- **The U.S. dollar:** This is far and away the top currency on the market. America has the world's largest economy at this time and every bank across the planet has the largest chunk of its foreign exchange reserves held in its currency. It's perceived as safe precisely because it is the bedrock of the biggest economy in the world and also because it is backed by the Federal Reserve. Also, commodities such as gold and energy products are priced in U.S. dollars. You'll notice quite quickly that traders tend to scurry back towards the dollar in times of uncertainty because it's seen as the safest possible place to store money. It's also the place for low risk trading, which in turn will of course net lower profits. As a new trader, the U.S. dollar is the one you should always be watching, because the majority of the time it will tell you what's happening in the rest of the market. When it goes up, everything else generally goes down. Keep an eye on the U.S. dollar index to see what's happening with this currency – it's your starting point and also your anchor point as you venture through the world of Forex trading. To do this, simply look for the FXCM index on the internet, which compares the dollar against three other currencies: the British pound, the Australian dollar and the Japanese yen.

- **The Euro:** Obviously, a currency that covers half a continent is going to be very important. It's never been the most stable of currencies thanks to the constant machinations of the European nations and their combined Union and there is always talk of it eventually collapsing, sooner or later. Huge events such as the Brexit vote in the United Kingdom tend to have large impacts on this currency and smaller events in individual countries also affect it – and these happen often, making it volatile to say the least. The actual effects can be strange and unexpected, all of which leads to the Euro being perceived as a high risk currency for investors. Nevertheless, it's the second most widely held currency in the world's banks, after the U.S. dollar, and is therefore an important part of the market.

- **British pound:** Britain opted not to join the Euro when it entered into the European Union and so the pound – the world's oldest currency still in use today, having been around since the eighth century – is still going strong. Except in times of great turmoil, as we saw with the Brexit vote, it tends to be stable and steady with very few moments of volatility. As London is still considered to be the financial capital of the world, it's usually viewed to be among the safe currencies. The GBP tends to waver much less according to politicking than other currencies so you'll notice that events themselves have exactly the effect you'd expect on it, making it go up and down. This is not the case for other currencies; the Euro, for example, can be dramatically impacted by the political rhetoric surrounding an event as well as the news itself. All of this – particularly its predictability – makes it an excellent entry point for a beginner.

- **Japanese yen:** As with the U.S. dollar, the Japanese yen is widely regarded to be a safe currency for traders and is where focus tends to shift in times of uncertainty. The Bank of Japan also tends to step in more than most other national banks if there is a concern that the yen is growing too strong and beginning to threaten the country's export industries. Its overall objective is to protect that market and it will always do this when necessary. Bear in mind also that Japan is a country with very limited resources and therefore imports a great deal of its commodities such as coal, which means its currency can be affected by, and can in turn affect, the commodities markets.

- **The Swiss franc:** Just like the Japanese, the Swiss central bank makes no bones about intervening in the market if it feels the need. Switzerland also maintains the traditional perception of being the world's safest place to bank and its economy is heavily invested in gold prices. This is because its bank holds huge reserves of the precious metal to keep the franc stable, so the currency in turn reflects the price of gold.

- **The Australian dollar:** This currency is strongly dependent on the commodities market because Australia is a land of mining and energy resources. Note in particular that the price of gold will impact the Australian dollar strongly. Australia's trading partner is China, so any events affecting the economy of that country will in turn have an impact on the Australian dollar. The country's economy is often praised for its strength and ability to rebound after an economic crisis, so the Australian dollar has a reputation as safe despite the volatility of the commodities market.

- **The New Zealand dollar:** New Zealand is a big exporter of goods, most of them food based, such as lamb and dairy products. It is a relatively stable currency as the country's economy tends to be robust.

- **The Canadian dollar:** Another currency that is dependent on commodities, this time oil. As its largest export, oil is the bedrock of the Canadian economy. Its biggest trading partner for oil is the U.S. so it stands to reason that changes in the latter's economy will affect its own – as, of course, will any events or news concerning oil itself.

Getting Started as a Forex Trader

Before we dive into strategies and information gathering, let's cover the basics of what you, as a Forex trader, will actually be doing. In other words, you're going to need a trading account in order to access the tools that will allow you to make investments and, hopefully, come away with a profit.

Your first task will be to find a broker, which can be a pretty daunting quest thanks to the sheer number of them available. Be aware that the Forex market is not heavily regulated, so it is very possible to find yourself the victim of a scam.

The most reliable way to avoid this is to find out which companies in your home country have been registered as Forex traders by the government – information that should be freely available on your government's websites.

You can also find out if the Commodity Futures Trading Commission has received any complaints about that broker by visiting its own website, which would be an obvious red flag about the broker in question.

Once you've narrowed down your list to a few well regarded brokers, you'll want to find out more about them. In particular, you'll want to take a look at their trading platform to see if you find it understandable and easy to work with, you'll want to know what kinds of tools they have to offer and you'll want to ask about the lot sizes you will be able to trade.

Lot sizes range from 100 units all the way up to 1 million units, though the standard size is 100,000. Decide, based on the capital you will be putting in as you begin trading, what size units you need to be able to deal in.

It's never a good idea to sink all your capital into one trade, so make sure your chosen trader will allow you to spread those eggs around multiple baskets.

A final note on choosing a broker: make sure they deal in the currencies you are hoping to deal in. Not every broker is equal and some will exclude certain pairs, so be sure that you'll be able to trade exactly as you were hoping to trade before you make a commitment.

Once you have chosen a broker, you can create a trading account with them by providing identification and, once this has been checked, your bank account information. Once complete, this will allow you to make an online transfer to your new account with which to begin trading. With that done, you're ready to begin.

Currency Quotes and Pips

As a new trader, the first thing you are going to see is a list of currency quotes for the different currency pairs on the market. So what should you be looking for?

The answer is in the pips. While 0.0001 of a dollar is not very much money at all, it's in that last digit that most of the movement happens. (As a side note, the market does quote up to five decimal places in some cases, but the fifth digit is so small that movement can be misleading – stick to four decimal places for best results).

As a trader, you are watching the pips because these are your trading units, so the first thing you are going to look for in a currency quote is the pips in the bid and ask price.

You will, of course, also be looking at the spread – the difference between the bid and ask price. This will change throughout the day and between brokers, so it will be affected by the volatility of the market and also by how much trading is going on with that particular currency pair at the time of your trade.

When you select a trade and open your trading position, you will be doing so at a small loss because you will be paying a commission to the broker as part of the deal. You have now purchased currency at a small loss and must wait for the market to move in order to move past that loss and into profit.

For this reason, your best bet is to trade in currencies where there is volatility, but that movement is relatively smooth and predictable.

These are the fundamentals of choosing trades, but how do you make that choice in the first place? The reality of the Forex market is that, even more than with other types of trading, the only way to decide what and how much you're interested in investing is to develop a deep understanding of the factors causing those currencies to move up and down in value. You won't find these on the broker's trading screen – to figure them out, you'll need to cast a much wider net.

Fundamental Trading Analysis

When it comes to figuring out whether currencies are going to strengthen or weaken, there are two styles of analysis that you will want to pay attention to. The first of these is what's known as "fundamental trading analysis", which is based on such things as economic reports and news.

Starting Point

A fundamental analysis is the best place to start, especially as you dip your toes in the trading waters. Before you do, though, you might want to consider how much you already know about the countries of the world and how they are governed. This is especially important in the countries whose currencies you plan to trade.

So, before you begin your daily analysis, make sure you create a clear mental picture of the countries you'll be trading on. How is their government structured and what are its cash reserves and deficits like? Create this as a starting point and then move on to your daily look at how things are changing.

Economic Reports

As a trader, you will want to stay updated on the economic reports coming out of not only the countries whose currencies you are directly trading, but also from the countries who are involved in trade with those countries. As we mentioned earlier, for example, the situation in the United States can have a big impact on the price of oil coming out of Canada, so it's going to affect the latter's economy.

You can take stock of a country's economy by looking at its inflation rate, employment rate and economic growth rate. In the case of employment, as a general rule the economy is improving if there are fewer people out of a job.

Be aware that there can also be seasonal impacts on this rate; for example, many businesses hire extra help for the holidays or for harvesting times. Conversely, you may see an uptick in layoffs when those events come to an end, which can skew the numbers. It's also important to be aware that the raw numbers aren't the only thing impacting the market: there is also the expectation of what those reports are going to show and the reaction of traders depending on whether it's as good or bad as expected.

If, for example, Canada was expected to release incredibly low unemployment numbers and the report reflects low unemployment not quite at the level expected, it can actually weaken the currency. If it showed even lower numbers than expected, this might cause worries about interest rate upticks, which will affect stocks and also impact the currency.

Inflation has a marked effect because it can indicate what's happening to the country's economy – but it can also be affected by growth rate. If the economy is growing, it often means there is a demand for currency, which means the currency is valued more but can also mean that inflation is rising and weakening that currency. These factors are linked so strongly that it's impossible to consider them separately.

Along with these reports, you should also pay attention to other aspects of the country's economy, such as interest rates. Short term rates tend to increase when the economy is strengthening and inflation is deemed likely to increase, while long term rates are affected by investment in government bonds. It's for this reason that currencies like the U.S. dollar are considered to be safe havens: their bond markets continue to do well even when less stable countries are suffering.

Supply and demand meanwhile play an important role: when it comes to international trade, prices change constantly based on how much of that commodity is available and how much is needed. The more people who want a good that's in limited supply, the higher the price will rise. Movements in funds between currencies will reflect this fact and will also affect the demand for those currencies.

Finally, it's important to be aware that most of the reports that have an influence on the Forex market are released at very specific times; the first Thursday of the month at 1 p.m. in your time zone, for instance. As you become more familiar with analysis, you'll start to learn when these dates and times occur and you'll come to expect them. This is incredibly important because the release of a report can have an instant impact on the market, so it should also be borne in mind when you initiate a trade.

For example, if you decide to initiate a trade on a Thursday evening but there's a report scheduled for 8 a.m. the next morning, the third Friday of the week, you might find that the report itself pushes the pips in the opposite direction to which you were expecting, scuppering your strategy in the process.

A quick search on the internet will show you that there are a number of free calendars available, some of which can be personalized to your needs such that you're only seeing the releases that will directly affect your trades and you're seeing them in local time. You can use these to your advantage by simply taking a quick look before initiating a trade to check whether there are any releases scheduled that may change what happens to the currency you're about to trade in.

You can also use them to remind yourself when those reports are looming – you can be among the first to check them when they release and can make trading decisions accordingly. For instance, you might find yourself closing trades, tightening stops or delaying a decision to initiate a trade.

News and Media

On a daily basis, you'll find news stories that have an impact on your Forex trading decisions. It's easy enough to root out stories that talk about government finances, the economy and large deals made by giant corporations, but you'll want to develop a filter as you sort through all that information.

Don't forget that "experts" can often be biased and stories may also reflect the hopes of the individual telling them or the government they represent. Thus the news can be remarkably helpful in developing your understanding of the world economic stage, but it's also important to remain skeptical of what's being said and find yourself as many sources as you are able to comfortably absorb in a day in order to verify, double check and ensure you're getting a clear picture.

International Events

While not technically a "source", it's worth mentioning international events in this chapter because of the immense influence they can have on your trading success.

Take a quick look at the headlines in the world's newspapers today and you'll see that huge events happen all the time. As a general rule, anything that causes fear and uncertainty is going to have a significant impact on the Forex market – and on your own individual trades, too. You can't see most of them coming, but you can prepare.

These massive events can include natural disasters such as earthquakes and hurricanes; conflict from wars or terrorism events; and human created disasters such as the meltdown of a nuclear reactor.

It's not uncommon for a country to shut down its markets when a massive events happen for the simple reason that panic can often lead to a crash. It's a way to ensure that cooler heads prevail before disaster strikes the financial markets.

When the market is shut, there's nothing you can do about your trades – they are frozen for the duration and your orders will not be fulfilled. The best way to avoid this from having a severe effect on your capital is to make sure you always leave stop-loss orders to automatically protect your position even when you can't do so yourself.

Looking for Economic Influencers

We've looked at the sources through which you can keep an eye on the fundamentals, but, aside from watching out for major global events, what exactly is it you should be looking for?

There are myriad influences on the market and they're all happening constantly, each one pushing the market up and down of their own accord while remaining just one part of the spider web and thus influenced in turn by other influences. Some of these influencers have global impacts and some will only affect certain aspects of a single country.

Let's take a closer look at some of the influencers you'll be sweeping for as you analyze the fundamentals:

Government Policies

Laws and regulations that a government puts in place can have a significant impact on the market. The objective of these policies tend to be directed towards keeping prices stable, making sure employment levels are as high as possible and promoting the economy. Be aware that there are many tools a government can employ to influence what's happening to the economy, from new tax policies to a policy that aims to increase business activities.

Monetary Policies

Central banks handle interest rates and the supply of money. Policies are used to maintain control over inflation and make sure the currency remains as stable as possible. It's arguably much easier to keep an eye on these policies and predict what they will do to the market because they are aimed directly at the markets, so they have clear aims that will have clearer effects on your trades.

The Bond Market

The bond market is a huge piece of the financial marketplace and as such has a big impact on trends in currencies. Informed traders like to stay abreast of what's happening in the bond market because the way money flows in and out of it correlates with what's happening in the currency market and can be very influential in pushing trends.

Political Changes

The markets don't like uncertainty, and a change in leadership is very much a time of uncertainty. When a country votes in a new administration, it's impossible to be sure who will win that election and what policies they will aim to fulfill. For the most part, you'll find that the volatility increases for that currency while the election is ongoing and for a certain amount of time afterward, until the new administration has made its intentions clear.

Interventions

We've mentioned already that central banks in certain countries can be a lot more hands on than in others. In truth, most central banks are willing to get involved if the currency is spiraling in one direction or the other, though some more than others. It's worth knowing how hands on the central banks are in the countries you'll be dealing with, because an intervention will adjust the volatility and impact the currency dramatically.

Market Ratings

Certain financial service companies are tasked with analyzing a country's finances and rating them accordingly. A triple-A rating ("AAA") means that the country has the capacity to meet its financial commitments; the lower the rating, the less they are believed able to do this. When ratings are released, they can significantly impact the economy of the country. A downgrade will have a negative impact, while an upgrade will have a positive impact.

Business Activities

When huge companies deal internationally, there is always a need for currency exchange. To acquire assets, even make big trading deals, one partner will need to exchange their local currency to pay the other partner. This temporarily changes how much cash is available in either currency, affecting demand and supply.

Statements from Officials

When officials from governments and banks make statements about the economy and financial situation, it can hold great weight with the marketplace. Watch out for press releases and even the minutes from meetings, as these can change the marketplace almost instantly, especially if they imply changes and movements that had not been foreseen.

Option Expirations

Be aware that funny things can happen on the monthly and quarterly expiration dates for the options market. Sellers will be aiming to secure certain price levels, which means volatility that can have a knock on effect. The upshot? Avoid these dates for new trades.

Analyzing an Economy

The many economies of the world are in a constant state of flux. You now know where to look to find out where in a cycle they currently are – and make trading decisions accordingly – but what do those cycles actually mean?

When boiled down to the basics, an economy is either going to be in a time of expansion or a time of recession. In the former case, there is an increase in economic activity and gross domestic product, which means more disposable income and thus spending, better employment levels and more demand.

A recession is basically the opposite and will see a drop in economic activity that has a blanket effect across internal markets for such things as housing and labor. If this gets bad enough or goes on for long enough, it becomes known as a depression.

Within those cycles you'll find inflation and deflation. Inflation refers to the prices being charged for items and services and usually rises when there is more demand than supply. Deflation, once again, is its opposite.

Gross domestic product refers to the overall value of those items and services that a single country generates over the course of one year. It's what the central banks tend to use to analyze the growth of the economy, which means it's also the best place to look to find out whether that country's economy is on the rise or on the decline.

It represents how much consumers are consuming, how much investment and government spending is going on and how much exporting is taking place.

Meanwhile, the "balance of payments" can tell you how healthy the economy is in comparison to others in the world, and it can do so fairly directly. It refers to all international activities and is considered to be in a good state when the country is accepting more payments from other countries than it is making.

The financial account will tell you how many international assets the country owns by looking at change in ownership. The country's budget deficit – the amount it must borrow above its income from taxes to meet the needs of its budget – will also indicate its internal economic health.

In general, what all these things will tell you is how risky the market is at the current moment. An economic decline is a time for safe bets, so it's usually when you'll find traders turning their attention to those safe currencies we discussed. In a time of increase, they will look more towards riskier currencies, which include the Canadian dollar, the Australian dollar, the New Zealand dollar, the British pound and the Euro.

Technical Trading Analysis

The second way to assess the Forex market is through what's known as a technical trading analysis. Some traders swear by this as the only real way to make decisions; others dismiss it and rely on fundamental analysis instead.

Whether you choose to rely on one or the other is completely up to you – and, over time, you may find yourself swaying in either direction – but arguably the best way to ensure you're making the right investments at the right time is to combine the two. More knowledge is never a bad thing, after all.

To illustrate, keep in mind that technical data is all about analyzing what has happened in the past, whether it was last week or a decade ago. This can show you trends and overall movements but cannot make predictions about such things as massive disasters – there's no such thing as a crystal ball, even with the most careful of analysis.

Combining a technical analysis that gives you a decent idea of the way things are likely to move with a sharp eye on the news and other fundamentals can strengthen your knowledge and ensure you're seeing things from multiple angles.

Technical analysis is done mostly from charts, which your broker may offer as a package on their platform – if you are planning to partake of this type of analysis, this is one of the things it's worth checking before choosing your broker.

The charts in question are called price charts and they are essentially graphs that show exchange rates over time. Depending on the timeframe, you will see more or less information. For example, a chart that spans a decade is going to show a fairly flat line over time, but if you zoom further in and look at a single year, you'll see much more movement up and down.

That time frame is very important, because as a Forex trader one of your biggest considerations is the time frame across which you want to trade. You are looking for the best time to make your play – the moment when a trend starts moving in one direction or the other – and for that you will need to be looking at the daily charts and predicting whether or not the trend you're seeing will continue or reverse within the next few hours.

You'll find that these charts include what's known as the moving average, which allows you to see trends more clearly. However, be aware that these are intended to smooth out anomalies and blips, in essence, and therefore may mask a vital indicator that things are about to change.

As a beginner, you'll be looking at the simple moving average, which calculates from a set of price points by adding them together and then dividing the outcome by the number of points you chose. A good number of points for this is 20.

Advanced Forex traders more often use the weighted moving average, which gives more weight to the most recent trades that impact the trend.

So what can those charts show you?

- **Support and Resistance:** Over the course of a day, it's usual for a currency pair to bounce up and down between a high and low level. The low level is the support and the high level is the resistance. This happens because traders are buying then selling currency to take advantage of the pip changes along the way, which you can do too. When a currency pair hits the support, you can buy into it, then wait as it rises to the resistance and sell. To do this effectively, you will want to make sure you place protection orders in case of unexpected changes. The support and resistance strategy is fairly effective simply because everyone is doing it. And because everyone is doing it, they are causing those plateaus to happen – they sell at the moment when the currency is expected to dip again, causing it to dip as expected, and buy when they expect it to rise, causing it to rise.

- **Breakout Trends:** These are the trends that break out of the support and resistance curve and generally happen in response to an event or a piece of news. You can use your economic knowledge to determine whether it's likely to cause the breakout to be upwards or downwards and make your purchasing and selling decisions accordingly. Patterns within the price charts will also help determine this.

Determining Currency Strength and Weakness

When you make a trade because a currency pair is rising on the market, it's important that you know how to figure out which of the two currencies is making this happen. Is the Canadian dollar driving the U.S. dollar upwards, or is it the other way round? The same goes for trades made on falling pairs.

It's not an obvious relationship to work out, but you're obviously going to want to know which of the two is the driving force. How can you do that?

Take a look at the currency matrix, which combines several charts to give you a picture of what's currently happening on the market. Use it to take a look at other currency pairs in which these currencies appear.

You might see, for example, that the Canadian dollar is rising in many of the pairs it appears in, which suggests it is the driving force. You can also see whether this movement is happening across every pair it appears in or most of them.

If it's only happening across some, this might mean that there isn't as much momentum to the rise as you thought, which could inform you as to whether it's a trade you want to enter into. You can also make decisions as to whether you want to stick with the pair you were planning to trade or switch to a currency pair where that movement is having an even bigger effect.

The Nuts and Bolts of Forex Trading

Before we take a look at the strategies you can follow as a new Forex trader, it's important that you know about the types of trade you can actually initiate. It's not too different to other types of market trading but, if you're entirely new to the concept, it's worth knowing what they are:

- **Market Orders:** This is a simple trade at the current price of the market. It refers either to a purchase or a sale, so you might simply be purchasing an amount of GDP at the price the market has it against the USD at that moment, or you might be selling it instead.

- **Buy Stop/Sell Stop:** This type of trade follows the trend of the market at the moment the trade is initiated. You are setting an order to either buy or sell currency when the price reaches a certain level. So, for example, you are placing a buy order above the current price and that order will be fulfilled when the price rises to hit that specific number. Or, you are placing a sell order below the current price and that order will be fulfilled when the price falls

56

to hit that specific number.

- **Buy Limit/Sell Limit:** This type of trade goes against trends and is what you would choose if you are expecting that trend to reverse. A buy limit involves placing a buy order below current price because you are expecting it to drop down to that level before heading back up. A sell order is the same idea but above current price.

Now, as a beginner, it might seem contrary to common sense to trade on both sides of the market: to make trades when the curve is heading down as well as up. It makes sense to buy low and sell high, so that's usually what we feel comfortable sticking with.

In Forex trading, however, there is plenty of profit to be made in a falling market. You can sell at the current price and then buy it back when it hits a lower price – you can do this even though you're selling something you don't actually own. It doesn't seem logical, but it's how the market works and perfectly legitimate. It's essentially just the mirror opposite of the "buy low, sell high" strategy and works in exactly the same way.

It's vital that you understand this tricky concept not just because it opens up the full market to you and makes sure you're not ignoring events and movements that are potentially very profitable, but also because the downward slope is usually much quicker than the upward. A falling market therefore allows you to make your profits much more quickly.

Another very important concept for a new trader is the idea of leverage. This refers to the practice of borrowing from your broker in order to increase your ability to make a profit. By using credit, you can buy more currency, which means you'll have more to sell, which means you'll make more profit when you do.

It's a tempting idea, but it has a very big downside. If you wipe out your account and borrow more from your broker on what you believe to be a sure bet, only to see it fail, then you don't end the trade just with empty pockets – you end it owing money.

That's not to say it's something you should rule out. The more you put into a trade, the more you get out of it, so in the case of "sure bets" and safer currency pairs, it can be remarkably fruitful. However, if you do make use of leverage (and every broker will allow a different level of leverage, so it's worth finding that out when you pick your broker), be very aware indeed of the risk you are taking.

Another aspect of trading that it's important to understand is contract sizes. When you make a trade on the market, you are not actually buying or selling raw currency. You are buying or selling a contract that promises delivery of that amount of currency.

A contract deals in "lots", which is the amount of one currency you'll be trading in the deal. A "mini lot" is ten times bigger than a "micro lot" and a "lot" is ten times bigger than a "mini lot". In other words, a micro lot might involve 1000 units of currency, a mini lot 10,000 units of currency and a lot would be 100,000 units. As an individual trader, you will likely be dealing in mini lots, but micro lots can be an excellent starting point while you learn how to tackle the Forex market – less potential loss, more individual trades to play with.

The Importance of Pips

You might be thinking that it's going to take some significant changes in the market price to earn you a profit, but actually that's not the case. The amount by which currency pairs move over the course of the day is greater than you might think; for major pairs, it can move up to 120 pips in a single day. Within that range are plenty of opportunities for you to make a profit.

But what number of pips should you personally be aiming for? In other words, how much market movement should you be aiming to capitalize on in a single day?

One pip, when we're talking about profit, is equal to $10 in USD. As a beginner, aiming for around 10 to 20 of those per day is going to bring you $100 to $200 in profit if you are successful.

That might not sound like a gold mine, but it's going to add up fast over the course of a week or a month – it's basically the equivalent of an average wage for many parts of the world. Therefore, by aiming around this level, you could easily be doubling your income.

Of course, this is assuming that you've entered the Forex market on an average wage. If you earn less and have less disposable income to funnel into your account, it's worth thinking of adjusting your expectations downwards – at least until you can bolster your account with your profits. If you earn a wage well above average, you can play with bigger pip numbers and you can take bigger risks than the rest of us.

Now, what we are discussing here is simply a matter of setting up your personal goals. We are talking about a desire to earn $100 to $200 per day, not a reality. In actual reality, managing this consistently is not going to be easy, though it is indeed possible.

The real point here is that even an experienced trader should avoid getting carried away. It's all too easy to see good returns and invest more and more in one day, losing your profit and your account balance in the process.

The best traders set themselves a pip goal over the course of a single day, decide on the level of risk they are willing to entertain and then attempt to hit that goal, then call it quits if and when they do. This allows them to build their capital over time.

That's important, because the more capital you have, the more you can invest in any one trade – and, in turn, the more profit you stand to make. Your starting capital may well be relatively low. At first, this may mean sticking to micro lots as you build your capital. Then, once you have proved to yourself that you can trade with consistent success and you consequently have more capital to play with, you can switch to mini lots – and perhaps beyond!

Day Trading Versus Long Term Trading

There are two main types of traders on the Forex market. One deals in trades that open and close within the space of a day, others in the type of trade that is still open when the day comes to a close.

For a day trader, concentration is key – you'll be performing a lot of interactions with your broker over a short space of time and must be able to keep track of all of them. You may also miss out on big events and anomalies that would be worthwhile, because most day traders sit down to look at their trades for just a couple of hours during the day. The exciting stuff is not guaranteed to happen in that time, especially if you're in a time zone where it's hard to coincide with the biggest market movements.

On the other hand, you don't need to keep coming back to check on your trades over time and this can be a rewarding way to make daily profits within a short amount of time. You can also set tighter stops and you'll find it easier to manage your risk.

Long term trading scales up in every way. The trades, obviously, last for longer and meeting your risk level means increasing the number of pip stops you consider for your stop. Long term trade is also more risky in overall terms – the further out a trade, after all, the less possible it is to make accurate predictions.

It's up to you which one you are more comfortable with. As you enter into the Forex market, it can be helpful to enter into trades that have different time spans to experiment with what works for you. Give it time – one trade is never going to be the same as another. Spend a few weeks engaging in trades that run the full range of time spans and see how comfortable you feel with the risk, how well you are able to make predictions and how easily each type fits with your personal daily schedule.

Developing Your Trading Plan

You now have the fundamental principles of Forex trading under your belt and you are aware what you are trading in and why. So how do you translate that into a practical application?

Every successful trader enters the marketplace with a clear plan in their mind and the reason they can then describe themselves as successful is because they follow it dutifully and religiously.

Now, while it's true that you can find software out there that will make those decisions for you, I strongly recommend that you avoid the temptation. Much as with those crash diets that never help lose more than a couple of pounds and the wonder medicines that do little else than taste unpleasant, those software programs tend to be snake oil. After all, if they really did work, everyone would be using them and everyone would be millionaires.

Instead, you're going to have to create your own plan and then rely on your hard work to research the markets, your intuition and your ability to assess risk to provide the rest.

To get started is relatively simple. You will need to provide yourself the answer to two questions:

- What is the maximum loss you are prepared to make on a single position? (In percentage terms.)

- What will be your stop loss position on your trades?

Every trader needs to know the answer to those questions, although everything else is fluid and personal. Your ability to analyze the market, the time of day you trade, your capital and risk ability – these things are all distinctly personal, which means there is no possible way to develop a plan that works for absolutely everybody.

Not to mention that the same strategy won't necessarily work in every market and on every trade or with every currency pair. You will need to develop a fluid mindset that can adapt your plan accordingly to the realities of the market.

So, with that in mind, how do you develop your personal strategy? Start with the two questions above, as these are designed to make sure that the capital in your trading account remains intact. Answer those questions with a mind to your trading account and to how much you can afford to lose before you no longer have the capital to continue trading. Your answers are the only ones to which you must adhere religiously, come what may. Consider your capital to be your prize possession and worthy of protection at all times.

A quick example to show you how those questions then apply to an actual trade. Let's assume that you've decided that your maximum risk on a trade is going to be $45, which equates to 2 percent of your capital (I would recommend never going above 5 percent), and that you've decided your stop loss position will represent three times the average pip movement of that currency pair.

Now let's assume you're looking at a trade that moves on average five pips within your chosen timeframe. You would therefore have a stop loss position of 15 pips. If you divide the maximum loss you're prepared to make by the number of pips, you get the number 3, which translates to $3 per pip.

So what does that mean? It means that you want a contract that balances out at $3 per pip.

You can, of course, then play with your equation. For example, if you enter into a contract with less risk than you're prepared to take, you can then increase your position later if your predictions bear out, adding more contracts until you reach that $45 maximum. Don't forget that the answer to these questions represents the maximum risk you're prepared to take, so you don't actually have to meet those numbers exactly as long as you don't exceed them.

Step by Step Trading Plan Decisions

With those two basic questions asked and answered, you have numbers to play with that will guide you through individual trades. But what of your overall strategy? To develop that, you'll need to ask yourself some questions that you may have already been thinking about as you worked through this book.

1. How much capital do you want to invest and how much time do you want to spend trading? The decisions you make about your trading need to fit with your lifestyle and responsibilities, so it's best to work this out first and then develop your plan to fit around these basic needs.

2. How do you want to perform your analysis? You've been introduced to the basics of both fundamental and technical analysis in this book and I did suggest that a combination of the two is a good idea. Before you decide which to use, experiment with them for a little while. Make theoretical trades based on what you have learned through research and see how they pan out. Traders don't all use one or the other of these systems, and that's for good

reason – our brains all work in their own unique ways and you may find yourself making better decisions using one over the other.

3. What are your financial goals and targets? We discussed earlier that you should enter the market with a daily and weekly profit goal. It's paramount as a trader that you are consistent in your approach and making sure you have these goals will ensure that you are. As a quick note, your goals should be based on the number of pips you want to gain, not a solid figure in dollars or pounds. As your capital grows, you'll be investing in bigger contracts, so the pips will represent larger amounts of money. This is how you will grow your capital: by consistently following the same strategy as you go along and seeing how that strategy brings bigger gains over time.

4. Do you want to be a long or short term trader? This is going to affect how you perform your research and what you are looking for and, ultimately, will dictate what it is that makes you decide to enter into a trade.

5. What currency pairs do you want to trade in? Keep in mind the risk associated with each pair and also your personal circumstances – there's no point trading on a currency that's barely moving during the time you're able to trade, for example.

With all these questions answered, you must now take on board that all of your trading is going to come down to the idea of risk. It is based around how much risk you are prepared to take in general – the answers to those first two questions – and how much risk a particular position represents. If you keep this in mind during every trade decision, you can't go too far wrong.

Make those high risk choices if you want to, but make sure that you're aware they are high risk before you do and that you're not taking any greater risk than your plan dictates.

Basic Strategies for First Time Traders

Your plan, as we've said, is highly personal, but as a beginner there are a few strategies you can incorporate that will help you grow used to the market and develop your understanding of individual trades. It's those first few decisions that cause nails to be bitten down to the quick, after all, so there's nothing wrong with sticking to tried and tested ideas while you make them.

As time goes on, you'll naturally begin to experiment and adapt your decisions to your growing understanding. At first, try some of these strategies on for size, keeping in mind that they won't all work as well or in the same way for every trade situation.

First, a very basic step by step strategy to making sure that the gains you achieve are the best gains possible:

1. Begin with a limit order. This ensures you are purchasing at a set price and are not focusing on the market price, which will move up and down while the order is active.
2. Decide your possible gain in terms of pips.
3. Decide your stop loss.
4. Exit your position the very moment that you gain the profit you aimed for or when you hit

that stop loss. Avoid the temptation to stick around to see if you can make more or if the currency pair bounces back – remember, this is all about consistency and making precisely the number of pips you set out to make that day.

Now, a look at the methods that will help you avoid suffering huge losses in your trades. This time, not so much a step by step guide as three choices you have when you are setting your trade, which you can use individually or in combination:

1. A stop loss order: This is where you decide your worst case scenario. It's the high or low at which you will reach a loss that represents the maximum risk you're prepared to take.
2. A trailing stop loss: This can be a better choice because it follows the price and represents a certain number of pips off that current price. If the market turns, it allows your position to close, but if it continues in that trend, you can continue to make profit until you set a closing order.
3. A take profit: This order removes the profit you have gained while continuing your position.

Next, a strategy for analysis to help you get started:

1. Take a look at the overall global economic situation.
2. Now, narrow this down to the specific currency pair you have an interest in trading. Look for any information, whether it be a report or a news item or something else, that pertains to this pair and that could have an effect on the movement of that pair over the next few hours.
3. Look for support and resistance.
4. Look for any breakout trend indicators.
5. If you can identify three different indicators that suggest you should trade in a specific currency, go ahead and set your order.

Next, an overall plan that takes you through what to do with the charts at your disposal and how to use the simple movement of the support and resistance from the moment you sit down at your computer to the end of an individual trade:

1. Take a close look at the currency index. Use it to identify a currency pair that is showing good movement and is therefore worth investing in.
2. Look at the charts for that pair over different time frames: a year, six months, three months, one month and then the current week. Look for

patterns across those time frames that could be impactful to today's movement.

3. Look at the daily chart to find out if you should be buying or selling in that currency. Move down to the four hour chart to see if the indicators are the same.

4. On the hourly chart, look for the support and resistance. If you can see it, pay attention to the ten minute intervals to see how it changes.

5. Once you have decided which interval is the best one to buy or sell because the support or resistance level has been hit, make your position.

6. Set your orders and positions. Exit the position when the movement has traveled down to the opposite direction (the support if you started with the resistance and the resistance if you began with the support). Exit your trade.

7. Repeat this for the next interval. By continuing to do this with the best currency pair available to you, you'll find yourself hitting your pip target consistently and relatively easily.

Finally, a strategy that makes broad use of the available information and your options:

1. Choose your currency pairs according to factors such as which window of time you are

trading in and which are showing the best movement at this time.

2. Look to your fundamental analysis sources, such as the major news releases and the reports being released during this time frame. Use this to develop a clear picture of what is happening within the countries that may affect the currency.

3. Take a look at the currency strength indicator to look for strengths and weaknesses in the currencies, such as whether it is currently being over or under bought.

4. Watch to see changes in direction of a currency, which can often happen as other markets come online and represent traders changing their focuses. Be aware that any reversal can take time and can shudder before actually turning in its tracks, so the moment of reversal itself can be a shaky time to enter into a trade.

5. Using this potential trend reversal as a basis, look at the 15 minute chart and hour chart to find more information about the trend and more indicators of whether it will take place, when and how.

6. Decide whether you will be trading with or against the dominant long term trend. In other

words, if a currency pair has been moving downwards over the last few days but you plan to assume it will move upwards over the next few minutes, you're betting against the trend and the associated risk will be higher. This should inform you as to what trade you want to make in terms of risk and how closely you need to keep an eye on it in case you need to close it out in a hurry. A trade against the dominant trend is also rarely a long term position to take.

7. Now look at the currency matrix to see how those currencies are doing in general. This will tell you which of the two currencies is driving the movement you anticipate and how much trade is going on right now within those currencies. Once you have identified which of the currencies is driving the movement, look to see how it's doing against other currencies and use this to determine whether that movement is solid or risky according to whether it's affecting all currency pairs your chosen currency is involved in or just some of them.

8. Set your trade with a stop loss that keeps the data you've gathered in mind. The more chance there is of the trend turning on a dime,

the riskier your position is and the tighter your stop loss position should be.

The more used to Forex trading you become, the more you will find yourself moving back and forth across all these available charts, looking for signals and then backing up your finds with additional data. The steps above are very basic and give you an idea of where you should be looking, but don't be afraid to spend time on those charts and make predictions, then back them up, over and over again without ever making a trade, just to get used to the analysis part of the equation.

This is particularly important because the market moves fast – too fast for a beginner to really have time to figure out what they are looking at. By the time you've finished working out what's going to happen, chances are that it already has. That's just a question of familiarity, however, so you'll be doing yourself a favor by indulging in some "practice runs" to build that familiarity. The more you know, the better you'll do, after all.

It's also important to bear in mind that, while I can give you the basics of how to use all those charts and nuggets of information to your advantage, there is no single golden strategy that will make your trading successful. If there were, then every trader would be swimming in dollar bills right now. To be a good trader, you will need to be flexible and learn to use all these pieces of information to carefully analyze what's happening and make your decisions accordingly.

The key, therefore, to a successful strategy does not lie in the specific trades you choose to make. It lies in how you choose to analyze your market and use the information available to you.

By now, you may be seeing more clearly why I advocate for a split analysis strategy that absorbs as much of the available data as possible. For instance, looking at the fundamental data might show you that something big is taking place in Japan, and this in turn is likely to affect its trading partners. Turning your attention to the charts, you can see more closely what that effect has turned out to be and what that market portion is likely to do in the near future.

How much analysis you do depends on how much time you have available for your Forex trading, but I predict you will find that, the more you build in to your trading hours, the bigger your smile will be when you end your trading day.

In Conclusion

One last thing before you set out on your own explorations of the Forex market. A couple of reminder tips to help keep your capital safe when it comes time to hit that button and set your first trades into motion.

- Always, always, always include a stop loss order in your trade. This is one of the basic components of a trade and the most important, because it protects you from excess risk. For a short position, place it above the market. For a long position, place it below. That way, if the market does not follow your desires, you are protected.

- Do not ever move that stop loss order in the opposite direction to your position. You can move it in the same direction, by all means, if you want to increase your profits, but to move it in the opposite direction you are caving to fear.

- Use the same information you used to help you open a position to decide when it's time to close that position. For example, keep an eye on what the volume price analysis is saying about the market's movement, use the currency matrix to decide whether the currencies you are trading in are strong or weak, use the currency strength indicator to look for trends and keep an eye on the news to see what major developments are happening.

Forex trading is a very personal journey that begins and ends with your analysis. There is no right or wrong answer when you're deciding how to make the market work for you – perhaps you'll be happy as a short term trader, maybe you prefer to be long term; perhaps you prefer one style of analysis to another and find that you make better decisions when you rely on a specific combination.

The only golden rule is to remember your risk levels and always stick to them, come what may. Maintain that capital and it will always be there to work for you, earning you those small but consistent profits that, over time, can build into an incredible nest egg.

Practice makes perfect, so go ahead and experiment as you dip your toes in the water. If you have capital to spare, feel free to experiment with real money and real trades. If you prefer to be more cautious, there is absolutely nothing wrong with the idea of "pretend trades" before you risk your real savings.

However you choose to get started, keep your focus on analysis and on sticking to your risk levels and you'll see those profits begin to stack up before you know it.

Special Thanks

I would like to give special thanks to all the readers from around the globe who chose to share their kind and encouraging words with me.

Knowing even just one person found this book helpful means the world to me.

If you've benefited from this book at all, I would be honored to have you share your thoughts on it, so that others would get something valuable out of this book as well.

Your reviews are the fuel for my writing soul, and I'd be **<u>forever grateful</u>** to see *your* review, too.

Thank you all.